JORDAN PEELE

AND

KEEGAN-MICHAEL KEY

THE GIANTS OF COMEDY™

JORDAN PEELE AND KEEGAN-MICHAEL KEY

VANESSA OSWALD

Rosen YA™

New York

Published in 2020 by The Rosen Publishing Group, Inc.
29 East 21st Street, New York, NY 10010

First Edition

Library of Congress Cataloging-in-Publication Data

Names: Oswald, Vanessa, author.
Title: Jordan Peele and Keegan-Michael Key / Vanessa Oswald.
Description: First edition. | New York : Rosen YA, 2020. | Series: The giants of comedy | Audience: Grades 7–12. | Includes bibliographical references and index.
Identifiers: LCCN 2018049559| ISBN 9781508188643 (library bound) | ISBN 9781508188636 (paperback)
Subjects: LCSH: Peele, Jordan, 1979– —Juvenile literature. | Key, Keegan-Michael, 1971– —Juvenile literature. | African American comedians—United States—Biography—Juvenile literature.
Classification: LCC PN2287.P36 O89 2020 | DDC 792.7/60280922 [B]—dc23
LC record available at https://lccn.loc.gov/2018049559

Manufactured in China

On the cover: Shown here with their 2016 Emmy, Keegan-Michael Key (*left*) and Jordan Peele (*right*) have proven to be an enduring comedy duo and so much more.

CONTENTS

Introduction

Comedy has gone through many transitions over the years. Each generation has had their favored comedic teams responsible for bringing laughter and joy into the hearts of many: the Three Stooges, Abbott and Costello, the Marx Brothers, Monty Python, Carol Burnett and Friends, Cheech and Chong, the Blues Brothers, Flight of the Conchords, Fred Armisen and Carrie Brownstein, Amy Poehler and Tina Fey, and most recently, Keegan-Michael Key and Jordan Peele.

Key and Peele's joint comedy touches on different topics in society, creating an objective and useful dialogue about things such as racial equality, gender roles, feminism, politics, and other social issues. Many of these subjects can be tough to talk about, especially for people of opposing political viewpoints. However, discussing these subjects through humor can bring a level of transparency to the important underlying issues. Through punch lines, people can find common ground and look at the world from multiple perspectives.

When Key and Peele first met, they had both played numerous characters and participated in funny skits and bits of all kinds with other performers. They had built their brands of comedy apart from each other. They stumbled upon each other during their time at the Second City comedy theater and school of improvisation in Chicago, Illinois, and each was immediately impressed with the other.

Key and Peele's Barack Obama and Luther sketches became increasingly popular during Obama's presidency.

Once this mutual admiration took hold, they became inseparable and combined their improvisational skills to form a comedy duo like no other.

After being featured on a variety of comedy and entertainment television shows, the pair eventually created a show of their own called *Key & Peele*, in which they no longer had to follow the vision of other directors and were in control of the content. They were also able to directly showcase their specific comedic abilities—not only independently, but also together. Most of the characters portrayed by Key and Peele on the show are fictional. However, some are satirical parodies of real people—one of those people being Barack Obama, played by Peele.

As Peele has become one of the best-known impersonators of Obama, Key's fictional character of Obama's anger translator, named Luther, is equally well known. Luther's comedic angle is to give voice to the angry thoughts Obama might actually want to speak out loud, but cannot, since he is so straitlaced. This routine became so popular, in fact, that in 2012, Obama met the comedy duo and complimented Peele on his impeccable impression and told Key, "I need a Luther."

Key and Peele both worked their way up from doing improvisational comedy (or improv) at Second City to performing skits on comedy sketch television shows to having their own wildly popular program. Throughout all of these experiences, they have amused audiences while also posing crucial questions about society within their comedy. They have also formed an unforgettable comedy bond, which fans were sad to see end when *Key & Peele* aired its last episode in 2015.

Speaking on their bond as comic partners to *CBS Sunday Morning* in 2014, Key said, "It's closer than friendship. It is a marriage, in the way that a marriage is a partnership," while Peele added, "We have to exist in each other's brains." As many comedy partnerships have faded out, Key and Peele seem to have lasting power and the talents to keep evolving through their comedy. As long as there is funny out in the world, Key and Peele will find it.

CHAPTER
ONE

Life Before Comedy

Despite growing up in different parts of the country, Key and Peele had similar childhoods, shaping how they turned out as adults. Their similar experiences also made it easy for them to relate and develop complementary approaches to comedy, focusing on subjects that affected them both. They would not meet until their time at Second City, when they were young adults, but it was their formative years that influenced their personalities and encouraged them to bond.

Baby Key

Keegan-Michael Key was born in Southfield, Michigan, on March 22, 1971. He spent most of his childhood growing up around Detroit, Michigan. Patricia Walsh and Michael Key adopted him at a young age. His adoptive mother is white and his adoptive father is black, and both were social workers. After adopting Keegan-Michael, his adoptive parents had a biological son as well. The couple eventually divorced when he was an adolescent, and his adoptive father got remarried to Margaret McQuilllian-Key, a white woman from Northern Ireland.

One of Key's first ambitions was to grow up to be a veterinarian. He also dreamed of being a movie star or becoming a football player. However, he was diagnosed with epilepsy, which kept him from playing football. Instead, he took up acting, which his adoptive mother supported wholeheartedly.

Keegan-Michael Key attended Shrine Catholic High School in Royal Oak, Michigan. In his junior year of high school, his choir director encouraged his acting and urged him to try out for a role in the school's production of *Godspell*. He ended up being cast in the role of Jesus. "That's what started it all," Key told Jack Walsworth of the *Varsity News*. "I remember after that thinking, 'Geez, I don't think I want to be a veterinarian anymore I think I want to do this.' Also, because being a veterinarian requires math and I don't do math. I enjoyed acting so much." When he was eighteen, his adoptive father and stepmother sent him on a trip to England to study drama after acknowledging how big a passion it was for him.

Though his adoptive parents took him in at a young age, they always told him he would have the option to someday meet his biological mother. At age twenty-five, Key met his birth mother, Carrie Herr, who is white. He found out that his birth was the result of an affair between Herr and her married black coworker, Leroy McDuffie. "That was one of the most unexpected and crucial and significant and foundational things that has happened in my life," Key told Tania Richard of ChicagoNow.com of meeting his birth mother. "She told me about her life and how she lives and how she made it through giving me up for adoption."

Growing Up Peele

Jordan Peele, born on February 21, 1979, in New York City, was raised by his single mother—Lucinda Williams—and grew up on Manhattan's Upper West Side in a one-bedroom walk-up apartment. His mother is white and his father, who left their family when Peele was young, was black. For the most part, his father was estranged from their family and died in 1999. "It's no accident," Peele told *CBS Sunday Morning* in 2018. "My art is exploring what the African American identity is and means. You know, not having my father around to guide me in what that means I think left me with a lot to question and explore."

Jordan Peele's first aspiration was to be an architect when he grew up. By high school, however, he dreamed of being a film director. Williams encouraged Peele's creativity by helping him make Halloween costumes and showing him a variety of different movies. He also spent a huge portion of his time watching TV shows: "Everything I do now, part of it is the fact that I had television as my second parent. Hours and hours," Peele told Zadie Smith of the *New Yorker*. Black fathers on popular shows, such as *Family Matters* and *Good Times*, were some of yong Jordan Peele's only examples of what a black male father figure was like.

Peele grew up watching the show *Family Matters*.

Peele attended New York City's PS 87 William Sherman School for grade school, the Computer School for junior high, and the Calhoun School for high school, where he graduated in 1997. In an interview with the Smith for the *New Yorker,* Peele explained how when he started attending school the first thing he was asked by other kids was, "Your mom's white?" Over time, he learned that other people were used to certain standards, and when something challenged their version of "normal," they asked questions. Explaining his biracial identity to curious people consisted of him having to "identify what I was or whose side I was on: Was I one or the other?" His mother also experienced strangers asking questions about Jordan being her son. She said they would "assume he was adopted or I was watching someone else's child. When he was still in a stroller, I would see people's faces freeze and then look away upon leaning in to admire the baby. You could almost see a 'Does Not Compute' sign light up in their eyes."

Comedians in College

After considering his options, Key decided to attend the University of Detroit (now known as University of Detroit Mercy) for college, which was close to where he grew up. However, one of the main reasons he chose this school was not the location, but because of the theater department's artistic director: David Regal. Key viewed Regal as a role model, who encouraged him to challenge himself when it came to acting. Regal admits Key stood out from the other students, as he told Walsworth of the *Varsity News*: "Like most students, he grew slowly.

SAY WHAT, PRESIDENT CLINTON?

When Jordan Peele was a teenager, he was given the chance to appear at the President Clinton: Answering Children's Questions event at the White House in 1993. The question he chose to ask President Bill Clinton was: "How can you help the families where there's a mom and she's taking care of a kid or kids and the father isn't willing or isn't able to pay child support?" President Clinton answered:

> If he's not willing we can have much tougher child support enforcement. I feel very strongly about it and I've got a good program to strengthen it. If not able and the mother is working and taking care of the kids, I think the tax system should actually give the mother money back if necessary. I think any parent working 40 hours a week with children in the home should not live in poverty. I think we should change the tax system so that people who work with children should be lifted out of poverty.

He did extra things that escalated his growth as an artist. He organized a once-a-week improv group on campus and ran it, which became wildly popular. He was aggressive in finding things to do in the art and

From his earliest days as an entertainer, Key was a hit, among both his peers and his directors.

pushing himself." He was featured in the school's productions, including *Talk Radio*, *Rosencrantz and Guildenstern Are Dead*, and *A Hero Ain't Nothing but a Sandwich.*

Key graduated from the University of Detroit Mercy (the name changed during his time at the college) with a bachelor's degree in fine arts in 1993. He next went on to graduate school at Pennsylvania State University, where he graduated with a master's degree in fine arts in acting, performance, and stage in 1996. After finishing graduate school, Key returned home to shoot an independent film—*Get the Hell Out of Hamtown*—in Hamtramck, Michigan, in 1996. While in Hamtramck, he also took on another project with his friends: converting the former coffee shop Planet Ant Café into Planet Ant Theatre. Today, the space has transformed into a large nonprofit artist community housed in a three-story building that contains several different branches, including a record label, a theatre company, and a film production company. In addition to performing improv at the Planet Ant Theatre, Key also started taking classes at the Second City Detroit after his friends encouraged him to audition.

Peele attended Sarah Lawrence College located in Yonkers, New York, 15 miles (24 kilometers) north of Manhattan, as a member of the 2001 graduating class. His intention was to study puppetry. However, his plan changed when he discovered improv thanks to his college roommate Rebecca Drysdale, who later became a writer on *Key & Peele*. After performing with Drysdale in her improv group, Peele was hooked. "I realized that with sketch and improv, I'm better than any puppet I've been making all semester," Peele told *Entertainment Weekly*'s Ray Rahman of his discovery of his talent for comedy. When Drysdale moved to Chicago, Peele came to visit her and saw a few shows at Second City Chicago. After this, Peele dropped out of college, having gone for only two years, and moved to Chicago to form a comedy duo with Drysdale. Peele and Drysdale came up with their own act called Two White Guys (even though Peele was black and Drysdale was a white Jewish lesbian). The pair went on to perform two popular sketch shows at

Shown here is a young Seth Meyers, who got his comedy start with Boom Chicago, where he worked alongside Peele.

Chicago's ImprovOlympic Theater (now called the iO Theater).

In 2000, Peele and Drysdale landed spots on the Amsterdam, Netherlands–based improv crew Boom Chicago, where they worked with Jason Sudeikis, Ike Barinholtz, Nicole Parker, and Seth Meyers. Meyers, himself now a big name in the comedy business, was deeply impressed with Peele's ability to write sketches. Peele's musical duets performed alongside Parker became fan favorites. One of Peele's most famous characters from this improv troupe was Ute, a stuck-up Danish supermodel who spoke terrible English. In his own life, Peele has experienced people reacting strangely to the way he speaks. Because he is biracial, he grew up changing his voice a lot. He believes this history of changing certain aspects of his identity has contributed to his passion for playing different characters, all of whom have unique personalities, quirks, and perspectives.

Code-Switching

Both Key and Peele have had to deal with being treated differently by people because of their biracial backgrounds. For Key, getting involved in theater helped him deal with being biracial. He told NPR's *Fresh Air* in 2013: "I think the reason why I went into theater, ultimately, was because that was one of those multicultural groups … it didn't matter how much melanin was in their skin."

Throughout their early lives, both Key and Peele did a lot of code-switching, which is the practice of changing the way one acts or speaks because of social factors. In the case of Key and Peele, it meant they switched back and forth between two races—identifying or acting like a black person or a white person, depending on with whom they were interacting and their social situation. A career as an actor, then, made complete sense for both Key and Peele. They had spent their childhoods code-switching, embodying other people's expectations.

Growing up, the two likely felt pressure from other people to code-switch. The people with whom they were interacting had their own preexisting ideas of what people like Key and Peele should be like, and code-switching is a natural way of "living up" to those expectations. However, constantly having to identify with two different races also clouded their own perceptions of themselves. It was a struggle they reluctantly endured, but later it served them well. As adults, they have used their unique, personal, and sometimes awkward experiences of growing up biracial as influential subject matter in their comedy. Not only did discussing this topic come naturally to them, but it also called attention to the struggles of biracial life for a person of any age. Key told *Esquire*'s John Wenzel:

> For me and Jordan, growing up as middle-class biracial kids and straddling two worlds and being told you're white and you're not black enough—or the white father saying, "Don't date my white daughter. You're not white enough," and not knowing where we belonged—that was our life.

For some, having discussions about race can be uncomfortable—but not for Key and Peele; they welcome it. As their careers developed—through stand-up and sketch comedy—they would learn how to talk about race, while also bringing humor into the mix. Through these jokes, they would make people laugh while educating them about race, racism, and the struggles minorities face.

CHAPTER TWO

Becoming Comics

For Key and Peele, performing in front of an audience became an essential part of life, and a way to share their experiences and talents with audiences around the world. Originally, neither had set out to pursue comedy. Both later came to embrace the art form while in college. Key had been a dramatic actor and found comedy along the way during his early performance career. Peele found comedy after his stint pursuing puppetry. While Key was regularly performing improv at the Planet Ant Theatre and Peele was performing improv with Boom Chicago, they both decided to take the next step in their comedy careers and head to the Second City.

Comedy Crushes

Key joined the Second City Detroit in 1997 and became part of the main stage cast, which included Maribeth Monroe, Marc Evan Jackson, Nyima Funk, and Larry Joe Campbell. Here, he made a name for himself, starring in eight revues. In 2001, he moved on to work at the e.t.c. Theater at Second City Chicago, where he was hired as a writer and performer. Here, he performed alongside castmates T. J. Jagodowski, Jack McBrayer, and Peter Grosz. "Second City was like me getting a second master's degree," Key told Yahoo! "I got to learn comedy there. Timing, how to write jokes, what the anatomy of a joke is, what the anatomy of a scenario is. It was one of the most impressionable times, and one of the greatest learning times in my life."

Peele came to the Second City in Chicago—with his castmates from Boom Chicago—to perform improv during a 2002 event. It was on this night that Key and Peele met, thanks to Drysdale, Peele's comedy partner and also a friend of Key's, with whom he had performed at the Second City. After Key saw Peele perform, he said, "This guy is my brother," he told Complex. Peele was also impressed with Key's improv skills, as he recalled his first impression of Key on Secondcity.com:

> All of a sudden, I am performing in the next room from Keegan-Michael Key, who I had heard about, but I had never met … He just has this energy like no one I had ever seen

and since in all of comedy. It's like, you know, there's a couple people who have that kinetic energy that somehow still feels true. And he had that. And, I was just in awe.

Peele played his vapid Danish supermodel character Ute, while Key played his high school gym teacher Coach Hines' character, who constantly berates his students. After watching each other

Comedian Rebecca Drysdale, shown here, was responsible for originally bringing Key and Peele together in 2002.

perform, Key and Peele went out to a diner with a bunch of friends and stayed out until the early morning. "I remember I went home and told my wife at the time, I said, 'Honey, I'm in love. I'm in comedy love,'" Key told Larry King in an interview.

THE SECOND CITY

The Second City is an improv comedy troupe founded in Chicago by Bernie Sahlins, Howard Alk, and Paul Silverberg (better known as Paul Sills) in 1959. Sills is considered to be one of the founders of improv sketch comedy. The first public improv workshops—taught by Paul Sills and his mother, Viola Spolin—were introduced in the 1960s. Some of the earliest students and performers at the Second City included Alan Arkin, Joan Rivers, Harold Ramis, John Belushi, Gilda Radner, John Candy, Dan Aykroyd, Catherine O'Hara, Eugene Levy, and Bill Murray.

In 1975, Second City premiered the late night variety show *Saturday Night Live (SNL)*, which was created by Lorne Michaels, who continued to produce the show well into the 2010s. The original cast of season one included Belushi, Aykroyd, and Radner, with Murray joining the cast in season two.

Every member of the early *SNL* cast, including (*left to right*) Jane Curtin, Chevy Chase, Bill Murray, Gilda Radner, and Laraine Newman, has become a comedy legend.

The show has earned more than sixty Primetime Emmy Awards and multiple honors from both the Peabody Awards and the Writers Guild of America.

The Second City Training Center opened in the mid-1980s in order to expand the number of workshops and education the theater could offer. Former students who got their start training and performing at Second City include Mike Myers, Stephen Colbert, Tina Fey, Amy Poehler, and Keegan-Michael Key. Today, Second City has theater and improv comedy training programs in Chicago, Los Angeles, California, and Toronto, Canada.

Becoming an Improv Artist

Both Key and Peele had to grow into becoming improv artists. Each of them had come from performance backgrounds, but the world of comedy was foreign territory for them at first. However, with the right guidance from other improv performers, they quickly learned the art form. Peele discussed training for improv on Secondcity.com:

> I like to think that any one of us can train and become a great improviser. It's almost like if you would imagine being born with a musical instrument that's unique to you … You know, someone can train a bunch of people how to play music, but you can only learn what your specific technique is and your style is.

Key shared the notion that engaging with his improv partners onstage and being there for them were some of the most important rules he had to learn to become successful at comedy. In setting up an improv scene, each performer has to rely on his or her partners to set the scene. The partners figure out where they are, who they are, and what they are doing by playing off of each other every step of the way, Key told King:

> Improvisation is about listening and it's about investing completely in the last thing that happened ... "What's the last thing that happened?" I'm simply going to retort about the last thing that took place ... Anybody can learn the rules of improvisation. You have to say "Yes," and you have to then add onto what the other person said. "Yes and ..."

If another person onstage barges into the scene unexpectedly, that can ruin the scene, especially if the original partners have not completely figured out their environment yet, according to Key. Eventually, once an environment is built, then additional improvisers can enter if the scenario around the scene makes it appropriate.

Sharing the Comedy Stage

After their original meeting at Second City, Key and Peele crossed paths again by chance when they both auditioned for the same available part on the popular sketch comedy show *MADtv*. Originally, the showrunners were going to pick only one of them, however, they decided to hire both of them after being impressed by their undeniable chemistry.

Peele joined the show's cast at the beginning of the ninth season in 2003, and Key joined the cast midway into the ninth season in 2004. After being cast in the show, they both made the move to Los Angeles, California, and were roommates for a short time. During this time, they played a lot of video games and analyzed the television show *Martin*. Key eventually got his own place, but the pair continued to enjoy a close connection, which was obvious on screen.

Some of the celebrity impressions performed by Key on *MADtv* included Ludacris, Snoop Dogg, Bill Cosby, Eddie Murphy, Kobe Bryant, and Lionel Richie, and female characters such as Phylicia Rashad and Eva Longoria. Original characters played by Key included Eugene Struthers, an enthusiastic deliveryman who sneaks into celebrity interviews to talk with them; Jovan Muskatelle, who sneaks up on reporters, interrupting other people being interviewed on the street; and the previously mentioned Coach Hines.

Some of the celebrity impressions performed by Peele on the show included Ja Rule, James Brown, Flavor Flav, Montel Williams, Morgan Freeman, Timbaland, and Forest Whitaker. His most famous impression was of 50 Cent in the parody music video for “Sad Fitty Cent,” which earned him a 2008 Emmy Award nomination. The music video features Peele playing the rapper as he moans about his rivalry with rapper Kanye West, who continues to sell more albums than him. Key plays 50 Cent's agent in the video. Peele wrote the video's lyrics, and he was involved in arranging the music, showcasing his versatility.

MADTV

The popular sketch comedy show *MADtv*, created by Fax Bahr and Adam Small, first aired in 1995. Originally, the concept of the show was inspired by the American humor magazine *Mad* (first launched as a comic book), founded by editor Harvey Kurtzman in 1952. *Spy vs. Spy* and Don Martin cartoon shorts were featured in some of the earlier seasons of *MADtv*, however, most of the show's sketch comedy did not relate to the magazine's content. Most episodes of the show consisted of sketch comedy skits, cartoon shorts, and musical performances. A lot of the humor was based around popular political, social, and culture references of the time.

Some of the cast members of the show throughout the years included Key, Peele, Nicole Parker, Ike Barinholtz, Mo Collins, Nicole Sullivan,

(continued on the next page)

(continued from the previous page)

MADtv featured many successful comedians over the years; this image showcases some of its talented performers.

Will Sasso, Michael McDonald, Alex Borstein, Anjelah Johnson, Stephnie Weir, and Debra Wilson. Some of the most memorable skits from the show included McDonald playing his character Stuart Larkin, an overgrown toddler, and Collins playing his screechy-voiced mother, Doreen; Weir's Dot Goddard, a hyperactive home-schooled seven-year-old; Key's character Coach Hines, who would constantly yell at his innocent students; and Peele's sad 50 Cent.

Show Biz Side Gigs

During their time on *MADtv*, both Key and Peele were also working on many other projects. In 2006, they appeared in "Weird Al" Yankovic's "White & Nerdy" music video. The song, which is a parody of Chamillionaire and Krayzie Bone's 2005 song "Ridin,'" is featured on Yankovic's album *Straight Outta Lynwood*. In the video, Yankovic plays an over-the-top nerdy white guy who approaches Key and Peele trying to befriend them. Key and Peele react to Yankovic by locking their car doors and quickly driving away.

Key and Peele played the roles of Woodsy and Kelvin Melvin, respectively, in the Comedy Central series *Chocolate News*, a satirical news show hosted by comedian David Alan Grier, which covered urban pop culture topics in 2008. They were also featured in the popular Comedy Central series *Reno 911!* between 2008 and 2009.

During the 2007 to 2008 Writers Guild of America strike—which put both *SNL* and *MADtv* on hiatus—Peele auditioned for *SNL*. The show was looking for someone to play Obama. The role was ultimately given to Fred Armisen until 2012, when it was passed on to Jay Pharoah. While Peele did not get to play Obama on *SNL*, he did eventually get to play him in comedic shorts on the online comedy site

"Weird Al" Yankovic, a comedy star in his own right, recognized the talents of Key and Peele before they broke into the mainstream.

Funny Or Die from 2008 to 2010, and then again—in some of his most famous work—on *Key & Peele*.

Peele appeared on *MADtv* until 2008, while Key remained in the cast until the show's final season in 2009. When their time at *MADtv* ended, they both took various smaller gigs in different movies and television series.

After a while, they both were tired of playing typecast roles, such as the "black best friend," and wanted to put their time and energy into a project with more substance. When Joel Zadak, manager to both actors, noticed they were going out for the same roles and both feeling unsatisfied, he proposed they create their own show together. Once again, the two performers would reunite—except this time more of the focus would be on them and their ideas, instead of taking direction from other people. They would have more control over the content and get to fully utilize their comedic connection.

CHAPTER
THREE

Comedy with a Purpose

Once Key and Peele met at the Second City in Chicago, they knew their instant and unique bond through comedy was special. While they had been featured in various sketches together on *MADtv*, they had never had the chance to fully explore this intimate connection and present it to an audience with a lot of creative control. After being a part of several other projects over the years, the duo was finally given the opportunity to be in charge of their own production, and what happened next is history.

Finding the Right Crew

At first, the two friends contemplated what they should name their show; eventually, they settled on simply calling it *Key & Peele*. However, there were other choices they almost went with, such as *Beige*. "It sounded silly or it felt stupid, because we were trying too hard," Key admitted to Steve Heisler of the A.V. Club. Peele added, "You don't want to try to get a laugh in the title, because if it doesn't work, it's the equivalent of taking a super-wacky picture. You don't want to put a rubber chicken in your mouth." The name *Key Versus Peele* was also suggested for the show. However, the two comics could not come up with enough topics on which they might disagree to fit the title's theme of competition or debate.

In choosing writers for the show, they went with some of their old friends whom they had met through comedy, such as Drysdale and Colton Dunn. Additional writers included Alex Rubens, Charlie Sanders, Rich Talarico, Phil Augusta Jackson, Sean Conroy, Andy Cobb, and Brendan Hunt. In the production roles, they hired Jay Martel and Upright Citizens Brigade (UCB) cofounder Ian Roberts.

For their director, they went with Peter Atencio, who was known for his Adult Swim shorts. He had also briefly filmed shorts for UCB's *The Midnight Show* and worked for Funny Or Die. Even though he was fairly new to directing at the time, Atencio succeeded at taking their show to the next level. His directing brought a cinematic feel to the sketches,

In gathering people to work on their show, Key and Peele picked many close friends they had worked with previously in comedy.

which was refreshing and something rarely seen in sketch comedy. "I'd rather direct short films than sketches, so we approached each one in the show like a self-contained movie," Atencio said to Natasha Vargas-Cooper of Vulture.com. Atencio directed every episode of the show until its fifth season, when Payman Benz also directed a few episodes.

Code-Switching Humor

After Key and Peele pitched their ideas to a few networks, Comedy Central ultimately picked up the show. The first episode aired on January 31, 2012. Key told Larry King:

> We just wanted to make the show as unique as we could. We wanted to make sure that all we were doing was doing comedy that made us laugh. In turn what ended up happening was that there's this weird voice, this interesting voice that people had not heard before.

That voice not only found humor in exploring subjects such as race, gender, politics, sexuality, and other social issues, but also created a useful dialogue about these sometimes controversial topics. Having a biracial background makes Key and Peele experts in discussing cultural boundaries and showcasing the different views of American people in relation to these complex subjects, especially when it comes to race. Key spoke to Ronke Idowu Reeves of BET.com on how their biracial backgrounds influenced them in creating ideas for their show:

> I do think our biraciality has a lot to do with how the show works. Mostly it's because …

> we're like racial referees in a way … We get the absurdities of both the African American subculture and mainstream culture and that informs how we look at comedy. It allows us to see things from different angles than a person who's wholly immersed in either one of those cultures might miss.

One of the main things the show does is present the various personalities and complexities within each race, often subverting or erasing preconceived racial stereotypes. Being biracial and experiencing people's different reactions, both Key and Peele displayed an innate sense of what it is like to assume many different roles based on how people expect them to act due to their race (or perceived race). This life experience gives them more freedom and versatility to explore unique directions in their comedy. Many of the people they have worked with over their careers have pointed to their life experiences as a reason why they are able to channel so much comedic talent.

In one of the first *Key & Peele* sketches, "Phone Call," which aired during the show's "Series Premiere" episode, Key appears on a street corner talking on the phone to his wife about buying theater tickets. Peele proceeds to walk out of a building past Key. As soon as Key notices Peele, he starts talking in a tougher voice than he had started out the scene with. Peele also talks in a tough voice as he calls someone up on the phone next to Key and says, "What's up dawg? I'm about five minutes away." Both of them nod in acceptance of each other and Peele continues to walk across the street. When he gets far enough away so that Key will not hear him, he tells the person on the phone "Oh my God, Christian, I almost totally just got mugged right now," in a higher, more feminine voice. This scene exhibits a perfect example of code-switching—embracing different characteristics associated with being black or white depending on the situation.

THE GROUNDBREAKING DAVE CHAPPELLE

Comedian Dave Chappelle's sketch show *Chappelle's Show* ran on Comedy Central from 2003 to 2006. His show parodied many aspects of race and culture, similar to the format of *Key & Peele*. In an interview with Gayle King on *CBS This Morning*, Chappelle said: "I fought the network very hard so that those conventions could come to fruition ... So when I watch '*Key & Peele*' and I see they're doing a format that I created, and at the end of the

(continued on the next page)

(continued on the next page)

show, it says, 'Created by *Key & Peele*,' that hurts my feelings."

Chappelle admitted that he is a fan of *Key & Peele*, but he also believes he deserves some credit for their show. Key and Peele have previously cited Chappelle as a major comedy influence. In an interview with GlobalGrindTV, Peele spoke about what *Chappelle's Show* means to him and its influence on *Key & Peele*:

> We knew from the very beginning that we had to do something different than [*Chappelle's Show*]. We knew that comparison was going to be coming, and … that's a tough one because that show is such a monster. It's so iconic … it is a big influence, but I think it turned out to be a positive for our show because … we can't do what could have been done seven years ago. We have to make these sketches … that we could only do now.

Key and Peele's show, ***Key & Peele***, had a format and themes similar to the Dave Chapelle show, *Chappelle's Show*.

Race Relations

Many of Key and Peele's sketches focus on blackness and whiteness because these are identities they have had to switch between, either out of their own confusion or because of other people's expectations of biracial identity. Atencio spoke with Vargas-Cooper of Vulture.com on how the show highlights these moments of identity confusion by putting them into a context that people will find funny, while also including deeper meanings:

> We're a show about race that doesn't take just one particular side. We're more interested in pointing out that ignorance and hypocrisy and stupidity exist in all races, so we use race to make universal points … Shows like *In Living Color* and *Chappelle's Show* were great because they brought a black perspective to comedy, and presented a voice that was underrepresented at the time. But we're not those shows. The guys are biracial, and that's apparent in the comedy and the character of the show.

While Key and Peele have played several black and white characters in the show, they have also branched out to imitate people of other races, such as Asian, Hispanic, and Native American. However, as they are playing these roles, they make sure to impersonate people of these races without mocking them. Their goal is to expose truths about identity confusion and cultural stereotypes as they relate to each race through playing these characters—their comedy is not based on putting other races down. They also are not afraid of bringing up the issue of racism and its prevalence in the United States.

In the sketch "Negrotown," from the show's final episode, "The End," Key plays a black man walking down an alley past another black man, who is homeless and played by Peele. A white cop passes by the alley and turns on his siren. He gets out and asks Key for identification. Key responds by telling the cop he was just walking down the street. The cop gets agitated and tells Key to put his hands behind his head and he proceeds to handcuff him and take him over to the cop car. While being lowered into the cop car, Key hits his head on the side of the car. Peele suddenly appears again and tells the officer, "I'll take it from here," and the officer responds cheerfully, "he's all yours," and takes the handcuffs off of Key. Next, Peele opens a door and leads Key through it. They are both transported to a place called Negrotown, a fictional place where black people can feel safe and free of stereotypes and racism. Peele bursts into song to describe Negrotown, and the lines in the song bring up police brutality, racism, and other struggles black people face regularly in real life but do not have to worry about in this fictional town.

Sketch Variety

While a good amount of the subject matter in *Key & Peele* focuses on discussing racial issues, some of it has nothing to do with race. At times, their content has involved commentary on politics, sports, relationships, pop culture, everyday situations, and sometimes, it is just plain weird and unusual—whether it is more in the realm of dark comedy or humorously nonsensical. "My gold standard is something that is so unbelievably dumb—but you're laughing," Peele said to Ray Rahman of *Entertainment Weekly*. "If you can get something to be so stupid that it's not even smart, it's the smartest kind of comedy."

One sketch that could be categorized as strange but comical is "Baby Forest," from "Babysitting Forest Whitaker," where Key plays a babysitter and Peele plays Baby Forest. The mother in the sketch warns Key that Forest is a unique baby but does not go on to explain why. Key tells her she should go have a fun night without worrying. After she leaves, Key sits down to read a book, and shortly after, Forest, who has the body of a normal child but

Peele's adult-sized head, along with a creepy, low voice, enters the room.

Key and Peele have also delved into discussing the rights of women and the LGBT+ community in some of their sketches. In their sketch "Pirate Chantey," from the first episode of season five, "Y'all Ready for This?," a bunch of grimy-looking pirates sing about respecting women in a variety of

On their show, Key and Peele would often wear wigs to transform themselves into other weird and funny characters they were playing.

ways regarding subjects such as consent for sex, abortion, and gender equality. In another sketch titled "Gay Wedding Advice," from season four's "Alien Imposters," a man, played by Peele, invites his gay coworker Gary, played by Key, over to talk to his family to answer their questions about how to throw a gay wedding for his cousin Delroy. Gary starts off by telling the family that a gay wedding is just like a straight wedding. The family continues to ask. After a while, Gary gets irritated and storms out.

Key and Peele are also known for their genre parodies, which are imitations of popular genres or characters from well-known movies, television, or cultural periods. Some examples of their genre parodies include their adaptation of the musical *Les Misérables* titled "Les Mis," a *Family Matters* sketch titled "Urkel's Revenge," and a sketch in the same universe as Hogwarts from the *Harry Potter* series titled "Inner City Wizard School."

While each of them have done impressions of celebrities and other well-known people on the show, they have also created some original recurring characters, such as Peele's Wendell, an awkward individual who still plays with action figures as an adult, and Key's Mr. Garby, a substitute teacher who pronounces all the students' names wrong while taking attendance. They also have the recurring

Key and Peele played funny characters while anchoring the 2016 MTV Video Music Awards.

characters they play as a duo, such as Andre and Meegan, who are a dysfunctional male and female couple.

Luther: The Anger Translator

While Key and Peele have created many unforgettable characters on their show, their most famous character duo is Obama and his anger translator, Luther. Throughout the five seasons of their show, they aired several different sketches featuring the pair. Key explained on NPR's *Fresh Air* in 2013 how he feels having a biracial president helped their show succeed:

> We actually felt like Obama was kind of responsible for us even getting a show in the first place, because there's this biracial person who might have to ride the divide between two different races. We know we're frustrated when a person like [Representative] Joe Wilson had screamed during that State of the Union address, when he was like, "You lie!" to the president. And we were like, "The president can't react the way millions of Americans right now are going, 'Ugh!' He can't say anything ... What if we had a surrogate who could get upset for him?"

In the first sketch, which appeared in "Series Premiere" and is titled "Obama's Anger Translator—Meet Luther," Obama, played by Peele, introduces Luther, played by Key: "I know a lot of people out there seem to think that I don't get angry ... So, just so there's no more confusion we've hired Luther here to be my anger translator." Throughout this particular sketch, Peele calmly and confidently makes statements about the democratic process, the governments of Iran and North Korea, the Tea Party, and the Republican Party, as Key repeats each statement much more aggressively.

Once word of this wildly successful sketch reached the real Obama, he was impressed by Peele's impersonation and also liked the character of Luther, joking that he could definitely use an anger translator. Eventually, Key partnered with Obama as Luther to do a comedy bit with him

Obama (*right*) and Key surprised the audience at the White House Correspondents' Dinner when Key came out to play Luther.

during the White House Correspondents' Dinner in 2015. For most of the bit, Luther is translating everything Obama is saying into angry outbursts. However, toward the end of the bit, Obama starts to express anger. In an attempt to calm Obama down, Luther says, "Whoa … With all due respect, sir, you don't need an anger translator—you need counseling. I'm out of here, man. I ain't trying to get into all this." The audience thoroughly enjoyed the routine, as they reacted with continuous laughter and applause.

Comedy Strong Suits

As demonstrated through each sketch they create, Key and Peele have become separately known for their different comedy styles and strengths. Key's brand of comedy tends to encompass more physical comedy, whereas Peele's comedy is generally more on the subtle side. "Keegan will surprise me with what he's capable of physically," Ian Roberts told Rahman of *Entertainment Weekly*. "I remember a scene where he had to jump through a window. And he actually just dove." Key admitted his comedy style is more flamboyant than Peele's, who is a bit more subdued.

Both Key and Peele assisted with the writing on the show, but Peele wrote between 30 and 50 percent of the sketches. "Jordan will lock himself in our office and knock out two scenes," Key said to Rahman.

Peele would then present his ideas to Key, and they would then build off of those ideas together, while also consulting the show's producers and other writers. In all, more than six hundred sketches were written for their show, but only half of these made it to filming.

After airing their last episode on September 9, 2015, some people kept inquiring if the comedy duo would ever bring the show back. In an interview with Trevor Noah on *The Daily Show* in 2017, Key explained why they had decided to move on from *Key & Peele*:

> The show for us came to a natural end … We just wanted to be so very British about the whole thing, which was like five seasons, let's get … out … You'll thank us now because if we would've gone seven or eight season you would've said, "remember when they were funny in the fifth season?"

Even though people enjoyed *Key & Peele*, the comedy performers knew they wanted to end the show on a high note. The show's ratings were still good and people were still interested in what they had to offer. However, if they would have kept it going for a few more years, they were not sure if that would have been the case. Once they had finished with *Key & Peele*, they went on to explore different

Despite the end of their show, Key and Peele have remained close friends and supported each other in their careers.

projects. They each also had more time to devote to their personal lives, which went through several transitions over the next couple of years. Through it all, however, one thing remained the same—their tight bond as comedy partners and friends.

CHAPTER FOUR

Making Things Personal

As Key and Peele navigated their way through the comedy scene, they were also balancing their relationships with their friends, families, and romantic partners. While building up their comedy résumés was crucial for both of their careers, they made sure to have enough downtime to maintain the bonds they shared with the people who knew them before they gained some attention from Hollywood big shots.

As each performer progressed on their journey toward comedy stardom, they met their wives, who were both working in the comedy industry as well. However, somewhere along the way, Key and his first wife struggled in their relationship and ended up getting a divorce in 2017. In 2018, he announced an engagement and later got married to his second wife, who works in film.

First Love

During his time in college, Key performed onstage at the Detroit Repertory Theatre. It was here that he met his first wife—Cynthia Blaise—who is a dialect coach for theater and film and has taught at Temple University, Wayne State University, and the University of Illinois. Some of the films she has worked on as a dialect coach include *8 Mile*, *Faster*, and *Bad Teacher*. She has also done some directing and acting. It was in 1996, as Key and Blaise worked on the movie *Get the Hell Out of Hamtown* together, that they formed a close connection. The pair started dating, and they were married on December 27, 1998.

After they were married, Key and Blaise were featured in Maribeth Monroe's "Meditations on Yoga: Ode to a Cougar" video short that was produced by Second City in 2010. In the video, Monroe walks into a yoga class being taught by Key. She waves at Key with a flirty smile and then gets bumped in the shoulder by Blaise, who walks past her. During the entire class, Blaise annoys Monroe by making obnoxious facial expressions as she is trying to get the attention of Key. Monroe starts to compete with Blaise and starts making similar facial expressions, but ultimately, Key's gaze returns to Blaise, which irritates Monroe even

Key met his first wife, Cynthia Blaise, when he was still living in Detroit before he found fame on *MADtv* and *Key & Peele*.

more. Blaise was also featured in a few sketches on *Key & Peele*.

After being married for seventeen years, the couple filed for separation on November 7, 2015, which came into effect on November 15, 2015. Following this decision, on New Year's Eve of the same year, Key filed for divorce. He cited irreconcilable differences when providing a reason for the end of their marriage. The divorce was finalized in November 2017.

Wedding Bells

A few days before his divorce was finalized, Key announced his engagement to Hollywood producer and actress Elisa Pugliese. On Twitter he celebrated, as he tweeted: "She shows me every day that each one of us has the ability to help make the world a better place. I'm the luckiest man ever. She said yes!" Pugliese has produced films such as *The Cake Eaters*, *August*, and *Better Off Single*. As an actress, she has also been featured in television series such as *Law & Order*, *The Agency*, and the films *School of Rock* and *The Cake Eaters*.

On June 8, 2018, the couple tied the knot at their home in New York City. The following day, they celebrated with a reception at One World Observatory. Some of the guests who were invited included Peele, Paul Rudd, Fred Savage, Michael

Strahan, Cobie Smulders, and Stephen Colbert. During the reception, Key joined the band onstage to sing his own rendition of "Tennessee Whiskey" to his new wife. After the wedding, Pugliese tweeted to Key: "Dear Mr. Key, I love you more every day. Sincerely, Mrs. Key." Key also expressed his delight to Julie Jordan of *People*, as he said, "It's a truly amazing thing when you can find someone who brings happiness and joy to your life. And more

After his divorce, Key fell in love with director Elisa Pugliese and they were married in 2018.

importantly helps you to share that happiness and joy with others. Before I met her I didn't even know that was possible."

Peele and Peretti

In 2013, Peele started dating comedian, actress, and writer Chelsea Peretti, who has been featured in several television shows, including *Brooklyn Nine-Nine*, *Kroll Show*, *Parks and Recreation*, *New Girl*, and *Another Period*. Peretti and Peele supposedly were introduced to one another by Peretti's *Brooklyn Nine-Nine* costar Andy Samberg. However, Peretti has said they actually met through a conversation on Twitter.

After dating for awhile, the couple got engaged around the time of Thanksgiving in November 2015. Peretti announced their engagement on Twitter: "My fiancé (lololol) @JordanPeele proposed to me last night during the family talent show lolol." Peele also tweeted about their engagement by posting a diamond ring emoji next to Peretti's Twitter handle on his Twitter account.

For their wedding, the couple decided to elope in April 2016 in Big Sur, California, with the only witness being their dog. As a guest on *Conan*, Peretti described the scenery of their wedding to host Conan O'Brien: "It's beautiful—oceans, mountains. We were married by a woman named

Soaring, like soaring above the clouds, and our dog was there, and that was it. No guests."

Peele, however, was the one who initially revealed that he and Peretti had tied the knot when he was a guest on *Late Night with Seth Meyers* alongside Key in 2016. The comedy duo admitted that working together has been enjoyable, however, Peele explained that some people are confused about which one of them is Key and which one is

Peele began dating Chelsea Peretti in 2013 and they eventually married in 2016.

Peele. From here, they did a comedy bit in which they are trying to help the audience discern Peele from Key. In doing so, Peele says, "I am married to actress Chelsea Peretti," and Key followed that up by jokingly saying, "I am not married to actress Chelsea Peretti. We're just dating."

ONE FUNNY LADY

Chelsea Peretti was raised by her mother and father in Oakland, California. She has two brothers and a sister. Her older brother, Jonah Peretti, cofounded Buzzfeed and the Huffington Post. In 1996, she moved to New York City and studied English, with a concentration in writing, at Barnard College. She started out writing for several publications, such as the *Village Voice, Details,* and the Huffington Post.

After graduating from college, she moved to Los Angeles, where she pursued writing for a variety of comedy television series, such as *Parks and Recreation, Saturday Night Live, Portlandia, The Sarah Silverman Show,* and the *Kroll Show*. She also made cameo appearances in a number of these and other shows. However, her big break into an

(continued on the next page)

(continued from the previous page)

Peretti played snarky cop Gina Linetti on *Brooklyn Nine-Nine*.

ongoing television role came in 2013 when she was chosen to play the quick-witted Gina Linetti on the comedy series *Brooklyn Nine-Nine*. Peretti went to elementary school with Andy Samberg, her costar on the show. Peretti, who has been on the show since its start, announced in October 2018 that she would appear in season six, but not for the entire season, and then would be leaving.

In 2012, she launched the call-in podcast *Call Chelsea Peretti*, where she listens to people who call in, and if their stories fail to pique her interest, she hangs up on them. Peretti also released her Netflix comedy special: *Chelsea Peretti: One of the Greats* in 2014.

Son of a Comic

The couple took their relationship to the next level when Peretti announced she was pregnant on February 4, 2017, by posting a photo on Instagram of herself revealing her baby bump. The actress also got to emphasize the fact that she was expecting by having her character on *Brooklyn Nine-Nine* also be pregnant. In one particular episode, her coworker Charles Boyle—played by Joe Lo Truglio—sees her drinking what he thinks is coffee and worriedly runs over to her and smacks the cup out of her hand. As he does this he says, "That could stunt the growth of your ... " and tries to avoid saying the last word "baby" because he does not want to assume she is pregnant without her saying so. This joke played on the idea that it can be very rude to assume someone is pregnant if they have not announced that they are.

Peele and Peretti welcomed their son—Beaumont Gino Peele—on July 1, 2017; a first child for both of the comedy stars. As Peele grew up without a father, when asked in an interview with *CBS Sunday Morning* in 2018 if he wants to be the father he never had, he answered, "I want to be the type of dad that my mom was." After a few months of getting to know his son, Peele revealed on *Late Night with Seth Meyers* in 2018 that Peretti had an easier time making their son laugh than he did, which he found funny, but says he also understands since he is "married to a hilarious comedian."

Brotherly Bond

After the success of their show *Key & Peele*, both comedy stars took the time out to strengthen the connections with the women they love. When they took a break from their working comedy relationship, Peele got married for the first time and Key got remarried. Their brotherly bond, however, remained. Even though their show had ended, they were still close friends and would soon start working on other projects together. When it comes to their collaboration in comedy, Peele said to Zadie Smith for the *New Yorker*, "We're brothers. It's not even best friends. It's a total brother understanding."

In moving on from their show, Key and Peele wanted to step out of their comfort zones and try new things. Neither of them had ever played leading roles in a movie, which is something they would soon tackle. Peele also had an urge to write and direct his own film, while Key wanted to return to his dramatic acting roots. As time went on, both entertainers got the chance to pursue new opportunities that allowed them to add new skills to their ever-expanding list of talents.

CHAPTER FIVE

Journey into Film

When *Key & Peele* wrapped up production, all of their fans were wondering what direction they would go in next, whether they would still collaborate, and how they would top the hilarious comedy they had already presented as a team. Luckily, new offers came pouring in for both comedy stars almost immediately after the show ended, and they both took full advantage of them.

As time went on, Key and Peele would take on projects separately, but also occasionally act in productions together. One thing that changed after *Key & Peele* ended was that they starred in leading roles in their first film together. Key, who had started off his career in theater, also made his way back into more serious acting—and not just in comedy films. Peele, who grew up with a love for horror movies from a young age, would eventually direct his first film in this genre.

A Cat Named Keanu

The duo's return to comedy after *Key & Peele* was *Keanu*, a movie about two cousins' search for a lost kitten named Keanu as they are also being targeted by a Los Angeles street gang. The film arrived in theaters in April 2016. Peele and Alex Rubens wrote the script for the film, which saw Key and Peele in the leading roles in a film for the first time. The name of the kitten was taken from the actor Keanu Reeves, who starred in the 2014 film *John Wick*. This movie also inspired the plot of Keanu. In *John Wick*, Reeves plays a retired hit man who seeks vengeance on the Russian mob for stealing his car and killing the puppy his wife had given him as a gift right before she died. Atencio, who directed the Key and Peele film, said they originally wanted Reeves to make a cameo appearance in the movie, but Reeves's representatives told them he did not want to take part in it. However, after a trailer for the film was released, Reeves's sister saw it and convinced her brother to get involved. When Reeves finally got in touch with Atencio, they managed to fit him into the movie, having him do a voiceover for the cat in one of the scenes.

The movie *Keanu* is a mash-up of comedy and action, comparable to buddy comedies from the

1980s and 1990s, such as *48 Hrs.*, *Beverly Hills Cop*, and *Thelma & Louise*, according to Key. While Key and Peele are the main comedy forces

Keanu was the first movie where both Key and Peele starred in the leading roles, and it was both critically and commercially successful.

in the movie, other comedy actors, such as Tiffany Haddish and Will Forte, are also featured in the production. Trevor Noah, who is a big fan of Key and Peele, told them during an interview on *The Daily Show* in 2016 that he hopes they continue to do projects together: "People love seeing you together … You're one of America's favorite couples. I see you on the screen and I'm like, 'I hope they stay together forever.'"

Return to Drama

Once *Keanu* was finished, the comedy pals disbanded to work on separate projects. Key began to work on the film *Don't Think Twice*, which was released in July 2016. This was a film about two subjects that are close to his heart: improv and the comedy industry. The indie comedy drama was written and directed by fellow comedian Mike Birbiglia, who Key feels wrote a movie about his life, despite the fact that they had never met.

The movie is about a group of friends who have performed in an improv troupe together for many years, and suddenly one of them gets a big break on a late night sketch show similar to *Saturday Night Live* and leaves the troupe. Key plays the role of Jack, the one who is offered a spot on the hit show, while the other friends are played by actors and

Tami Sagher, Gillian Jacobs, Key, Mike Birbiglia, Kate Micucci, and Chris Gethard (*left to right*) worked together on the movie *Don't Think Twice*, to which Key felt a strong connection, since improv was his first dive into comedy.

comedians Birbiglia, Gillian Jacobs, Chris Gethard, Kate Micucci, and Tami Sagher.

Key's next project was starring in the role of struggling writer Ethan Turner on the Netflix original comedy series *Friends from College*. The show, which premiered in July 2017, follows a group of close friends who went to Harvard together and are helping each other through their somewhat chaotic lives in New York City. Cobie Smulders, Annie Parisse, Nat Faxon, Fred Savage, and Jae Suh Park play the roles of the other friends in the series. The second season of the show is set to air in July 2019.

In November 2017, Key made his Broadway debut alongside Amy Schumer, Laura Benanti, and Jeremy Shamos in *Meteor Shower*, a play written by Steve Martin. Jerry Zaks directed the production, which was staged at the Booth Theatre and ran until January 2018.

Key, who has a background in theater, made his Broadway debut in Steve Martin's *Meteor Shower*.

After getting to return to more dramatic roles, Key finally got his big break in *The Predator*, which was released in September 2018. The science fiction action film, directed by Shane Black, is the fourth installment in the *Predator* film series. Key played the role of one of the ex-soldiers who bands together with other ex-soldiers to fight off the Predators to save the human race. The film also stars Olivia Munn, Boyd Holbrook, and Sterling K. Brown.

The Sunken Place

While Key was turning his focus to acting in films, Peele was exploring the new territory of directing them. He was working on writing a script for the horror-thriller film *Get Out*, which became his directorial debut. The film is about a young black man named Chris, whose white girlfriend, Rose, takes him to meet her family for the first time. Upon meeting the family, Chris feels welcomed by them; however, as the story unfolds, subtle, bizarre moments make him feel uneasy around the family.

The film uses racism as a main device in the plot and allows the audience to experience Chris's fears and uncertainties, which are representative of the anxieties felt by many black people and minorities globally when faced with racism. Peele said on NPR's *Fresh Air* in 2017:

It was very important to me to just get the entire audience in touch in some way with the fears inherent [in] being black in this country. Part of being black in this country, and I presume being any minority, is constantly being told that … we're seeing racism where there just isn't racism.

Peele's *Get Out* featured actors Daniel Kaluuya as Chris and Allison Williams as Rose.

In one scene of *Get Out*, Rose's mother has Chris sit down in a chair across from her while she sneakily hypnotizes him while stirring her cup of tea. She asks him about where he was and what he was doing when his mother died. At first, he hesitates to tell her but then surrenders and says he was at home watching television and that he remembers it was raining. She tells him to imagine the rain. The mother continues and asks him why he failed to call someone when his mom had not made it home, and he answers, "I thought if I did it would make it real." As Chris starts crying and reliving parts of this traumatic memory, the mother says to Chris, "You're so scared. You think it was your fault," and he says he cannot move. As he struggles, she says, "Sink into the floor." From here, he sinks down until he is floating in an abyss of dark nothingness, otherwise known as the sunken place.

In making this film, Peele, who is known for his carefully crafted comic sketches, had reached into a deeper part of his psyche when he created the idea of the sunken place, which is symbolic of marginalized, oppressed groups' life experiences. He said during The Envelope's annual Directors Roundtable in 2017:

> You know when you're going to sleep and it feels like you're about to fall, so you wake up? What if you never woke up? Where

> would you fall? And that was kind of the most harrowing idea to me. And as I'm writing it becomes clear that the sunken place is this metaphor for the system that is suppressing the freedom of black people, of many outsiders, many minorities.

Peele says in the movie, this particular sunken place within the film is a metaphor for the lack of representation of black people in the film industry, especially in the horror genre. In several horror movies, he noticed many of the black characters dying first, or not being represented at all, and in his own movie, he wanted to make sure the black character was not the first to die. Some of the scary movies he watched

HIGH HONORS

Both Key and Peele have won prestigious awards over the years, being recognized jointly for their show *Key & Peele*, and Peele individually for his directorial debut *Get Out*. In 2014, the comedy duo won a Peabody Award for *Key & Peele*. During their acceptance speech, Key said: "We'd like to thank Comedy Central for giving us the opportunity to show the African American experience as not a monolith, because it's not. It's so many different stories. The danger of the world sometimes is trying to assign a single story to an entire group of people."

At the 2016 Emmys, *Key & Peele* won the Emmy for Best Variety Sketch Series, receiving this award after the final season of their show. Both men were honored to receive the award and reiterated that their goal—which they achieved—was to spread awareness through comedy.

Peele made history at the 2018 Academy Awards after winning the Best Original Screenplay Oscar for *Get Out*, becoming the first black screenwriter to ever win in this category. During his acceptance speech he said, "This means so much to me. I stopped writing this movie about twenty times because I thought it was impossible." Despite the difficulties, he triumphed

Key and Peele won two Emmy awards in 2016.

(continued on the next page)

(continued from the previous page)

and made a film many people appreciated and enjoyed. After thanking all the people who helped him make the movie and the fans, he also extended special thanks to his wife, Peretti, and his mother, who he says, "taught me to love, even in the face of hate." When it was announced that Peele had won the award, no one in the building was more excited than his longtime collaborator Key, who stood up on his chair and yelled at the top of his lungs in celebration.

growing up that he said helped inspire him to make *Get Out* include *Rosemary's Baby*, *The Stepford Wives*, *Misery*, *Halloween*, and *The Shining*.

Opposing Racist Agendas

Both Key and Peele have been vocal about opposing racist agendas of all kinds. Since President Donald Trump took office on January 20, 2017, many people have criticized his leadership skills. Peele's film *Get Out* was released shortly after, on February 24, 2017. In an interview on *CBS Sunday Morning* in 2018, Peele spoke about his feelings for the Trump presidency:

> The president is a racist, which is very sad. I'm disheartened by policies that are xenophobic and sexist, and they're many strides backwards every day. What I am encouraged by is that the movie *Get Out* has been heard and received and that I'm seeing many other examples of art and film and television that are expressing these pains, frustrations, love in new ways and that they're being received and heard.

Key took part in a video titled "#StandUpForUs" along with other celebrities, such as Rosie Perez, Sally Field, and Steve Buscemi, to urge Congress to hold Trump's administration responsible if it seeks to do harm to marginalized groups. In an interview with Larry King, Key spoke about Trump's campaign slogan, "Make America Great Again," and how it is not practical. "The America that used to exist can't and never will," Key said to King. "If you try to wrest that back into existence, it's not going to work because history is against you. The browning of America is never going to stop." His hope is that seventy-five years from now a child will watch *Key & Peele* on YouTube and ask, "Why is this funny?" because the race issues they joke about in the show will no longer be relevant.

A Spike Lee Joint

Peele's next film project came as one of the producers of the film *BlacKkKlansman*, which was released in theaters in August 2018. The movie is based on Ron Stallworth's story of infiltrating the white supremacist group the Ku Klux Klan (KKK) in the late 1970s in Colorado Springs, Colorado. Stallworth was the first African American police officer and detective for the Colorado Springs Police Department. In making the connection with the KKK, he answered their wanted ad in the local paper that said they were seeking new members. He posed as a white supremacist and at one point even spoke on the phone with David Duke, head of the KKK, who apologized for a delay in Stallworth's Klan membership certificate. Stallworth posed as a KKK member for nine months, talking to other members on the phone—and when face-to-face meetings were necessary, he sent a white officer in his place. Once the investigation was over, Stallworth did not disclose any information about the case to anyone until an interview in 2006 with the *Deseret News*. In 2014, he published the book *Black Klansman*, which recounts his experiences during the investigation.

After hearing this fascinating story, Peele was inspired to turn it into a film, but his goal was to

Spike Lee was immediately on board to direct when he heard Peele's idea for the film *BlacKkKlansman* and thought it was a captivating story.

find the right director—and he found one in the legendary Spike Lee. He felt that the story had a lot in common with much of Lee's past work in films, which generally examine topics such as race relations, black culture, and struggles of the marginalized. "What's most amazing about [this story] to me is the fact that we haven't heard this story," Peele said in an interview with Flickering

Myth. "Not only is it so entertaining, but it's more relevant than it should be … It's one of these stories that the fact that it's been sort of buried is part of the problem with where we're at in this country."

Future Projects

Key and Peele have not been seen together on the movie or television screen since *Keanu*, but they do have collaborative plans in the works. One such project is *Wendell and Wild*, a comedy-horror stop-motion animated film where they voice the characters of two demon brothers who are trying to earn their way out of hell. Henry Selick, who has directed stop-motion animated films such as *The Nightmare Before Christmas* and *Coraline*, will be directing the Netflix original movie.

For Key's next acting project, he is voicing the hyena Kamari in the live-action remake of Disney's *The Lion King*, directed by Jon Favreau. Other stars in the movie include Donald Glover as Simba, Beyoncé as Nala, and James Earl Jones reprising his role as Mufasa. The film is scheduled for release in 2019.

Peele is also hard at work writing and directing the follow-up to *Get Out*—the horror-thriller film titled *Us*, which is scheduled for release on March 15, 2019.The film will explore the interactions and relationships between a black couple and a white couple. Some of the cast members already chosen for the film include Lupita Nyong'o, Elisabeth Moss, Winston Duke, and Tim Heidecker.

After releasing *Get Out*, Peele revealed he wanted to make four more social thrillers. "Each [social thriller] is meant to deal with a different human demon; a different monster that sort of lurks underneath the way that we interact with one another as human beings," Peele said, speaking with Kristopher Tapley on *Variety*'s Playback podcast. His production company—Monkeypaw Productions, which he founded in 2012—signed an agreement with Universal Pictures to produce a set amount of projects with Jason Blum, who produced *Get Out*. Peele's goal in making these movies is to help underrepresented minorities find a stronger foothold in Hollywood.

Peele's production company is also attached to projects as diverse as *The Last O.G.*, *Lovecraft Country*, and a reboot of *The Twilight Zone*. *The Last O.G.*, a TBS comedy series that aired its first season in March 2018, was created by Peele along with John Carcieri and stars Tracy Morgan and Tiffany Haddish. The show follows Tray, played by Morgan, who is released from prison early for good behavior. When he returns home to his Brooklyn neighborhood, he comes to find that it has been gentrified and that his girlfriend has married a white man named Josh, who is helping raise his twin children, Amira and Shazad. *The Last O.G.* has been picked up for a second season.

Peele is also executive-producing the upcoming HBO anthology horror series *Lovecraft Country* alongside J. J. Abrams and Misha Green. The show will be based on the 2016 novel written by Matt Ruff, which centers on Atticus Black, who will be played by Jonathan Majors. After Black's father goes missing, he and his friend Letitia and his uncle George set off on a road trip across 1950s Jim Crow America to try to find Black's father. This project appealed to Peele because, as with *Get Out*, this series reclaims the horror genre while telling it from a black American perspective.

The original *Twilight Zone*, which was a psychological horror series created by Rod Serling, aired from 1958 to 1964. A reboot of the series has been ordered by CBS, and Peele, Simon Kinberg, and Marco Ramirez have been chosen to serve as executive producers. Peele, who describes the original show to *Variety*'s Daniel Holloway as "a show that has always helped us look at ourselves, hold a mirror up to society," will also host the reboot, which is set to premiere sometime in 2019.

Searching for Truth

As Key and Peele started their careers together as dynamic comedic partners, this period of their lives

Key and Peele may collaborate again in the future, but for now they have their own projects to keep them busy.

has seemingly come to an end—or at least for the time being. Each of them has developed new creative aspirations and decided to explore these artistic endeavors. As a duo with a lot in common—from their biracial backgrounds and similar comedic interests—they were able to articulate several truths about race and inequality to a larger audience in a way that made it easier for the masses to understand.

In Peele's current role as a director, he seems to be working in a similar way to try to bring understanding to racial issues—but this time not through comedy. His work is exploring the same issues in a more dramatic way that comes from a deeper, more serious, and more personal place. Key, on the other hand, is soul-searching in order to uncover his own inner ambitions about what acting roles he would like to pursue next. After seeing

Peele get to make his passion project, *Get Out*, and receiving massive recognition, Key was inspired to dig deeper and ask himself what he really wants. "When and how do I reveal a new part of myself that's more intensely personal?" he asked himself in an interview with Yang-Yi Goh from *The Title*. "I've actually not done a lot of that. And when I have done it, it's masked behind makeup and a camera and a character in another person's story." Peele has also decided that, for now, he is done going in front of the camera and would rather be in the director's chair. "Acting is nowhere near as fun for me as directing," he told *CBS Sunday Morning* in 2018.

As both artists continue to search for meaningful projects, the work they did as a duo on *Key & Peele* will long be remembered, especially for its impact on helping society reckon with the complexity of racial issues. The show encouraged more open-mindedness about these issues, and the comedy made these issues easier to talk about on a larger scale. What lies ahead for Key and Peele is uncertain, but one thing is for sure—they will continue to pursue opportunities that speak to them on a deeper level and keep entertaining huge audiences every step of the way.

Fact Sheet on Keegan-Michael Key

Full name: Keegan-Michael Key
Birthplace: Southfield, Michigan
Birthdate: March 22, 1971
Ethnicity: African American, Belgian
Nationality: American
Parents: His birth mother is Carrie Herr, his adoptive mother is Patricia Walsh, and his stepmother is Margaret McQuilllian-Key. His birth father is Leroy McDuffie and his adoptive father is Michael Key.
High school: Shrine Catholic High School in Royal Oak, Michigan
Higher education: University of Detroit Mercy for his bachelor's degree and Pennsylvania State University for graduate school
Height: 6 feet 1 inch (1.82 m)
Favorite restaurant: Cadieux Café, in Detroit, Michigan
Favorite actor: Robert DeNiro
Favorite movies: *Midnight Run* and *Heat*
Spouse: Elisa Pugliese
First major film appearance: *Role Models*
First TV appearance: *ER*

Fact Sheet on Jordan Peele

Full name: Jordan Peele
Birthplace: New York, New York
Birthdate: February 21, 1979
Ethnicity: African American, English
Nationality: American
Parents: His mother is Lucinda Williams and his father left their family when Peele was young; his name is not available.
High School: The Calhoun School in New York City
College: Sarah Lawrence College (did not graduate)
Height: 5 feet 9 inches (1.52 m)
Favorite comedy sketch shows: *Chappelle's Show*, *In Living Color, Saturday Night Live*, *Mr. Show*, *The State*
Favorite movies: *The Shining, Gremlins, Labyrinth, The NeverEnding Story*
Favorite director: Stanley Kubrick
Spouse: Chelsea Peretti
Children: Beaumont Gino Peele
First major film appearance: *Little Fockers*
First TV appearance: *MADtv*

Fact Sheet on Keegan-Michael Key's Work

Comedy Troupes

The 313
Second City Detroit
Second City Chicago

Television Credits

2001 *ER*, "Quo Vadis," Witkowski
2004 *I'm With Her*, "Poison Ivy," Orderly
2004–2009 *MADtv*, multiple episodes, multiple characters
2008 *Chocolate News*, "Episode #1.5," Woodsy
2008–2009 *Reno 911!*, multiple episodes, multiple characters
2010 *Gary Unmarried*, multiple episodes, Curtis
2010–2015 *Childrens Hospital,* multiple episodes, Captain Tripper and Cop
2011 *A Series of Unfortunate People*, "Family Secret," Ted
2011 *Love Bites*, "Modern Plagues" and "Hot To…," Drew
2011 *Wilfred*, "Identity," Dick Barbian
2011 *The League*, "Carmenjello" Carmenjello
2012–2015 *Key & Peele*, multiple episodes, multiple characters
2013 *How I Met Your Mother*, "Something New," Calvin
2014 *The Middle*, "Hungry Games," Reverend Deveaux

2014 *Fargo*, multiple episodes, FBI Agent Pepper
2014–2015 *BoJack Horseman*, multiple episodes, Sebastian St. Clair (voice)
2014–2015 *Parks and Recreation*, multiple episodes, Joe
2014–2016 *Robot Chicken*, "Hopefully Salt" and "Stone Cold Steve Cold Stone," multiple characters
2014–2017 *Bob's Burgers*, multiple episodes, multiple characters
2014–2017 *Playing House*, multiple episodes, Mark Rodriguez
2015 *It's Always Sunny in Philadelphia*, "The Gang Goes on Family Fight," Grant Anderson
2015 *Rick and Morty*, "A Rickle in Time," fourth-dimensional being (voice)
2015 *The Hotwives of Las Vegas*, multiple episodes, Ace
2015–2017 *SuperMansion*, multiple episodes, multiple characters (voice)
2016 *Modern Family*, "Playdates," Tom Delaney
2016 *Angie Tribeca*, "Ferret Royale," Helmut FröntBüt
2016 *The Muppets*, "Swine Song," Keegan-Michael Key
2016 *House of Lies*, "Johari Window," Devin
2016 *American Dad!*, "Criss-Cross Applesauce: The Ballad of Billy Jesusworth," E-Money

2016 *Mack & Moxy*, "Buckle, Buckle, Seatbelts and Chuckle," Admirable Keegan

2016 *Bad Guys*, Mantis Commander

2016–2017 *Archer*, multiple episodes, multiple characters

2017 *The Simpsons*, "The Great Phatsby: Part 1" and "The Great Phatsby: Part 2," Jazzy James

2017 *Sons of Zorn*, "All Hail Son of Zorn," Grobos the Great

2017 *Jeff & Some Aliens*, "Jeff & Some Childlike Joy & Whimsy," Sauce

2017 *Detroiters*, "Smilin' Jack," Smilin' Jack

2017 *Samurai Jack*, "Episode XCVII," Da' Samurai and additional voices

2017–2018 *Friends from College*, multiple episodes, Ethan Turner

Film Credits

1999 *Get the Hell Out of Hamtown*, J

2008 *Role Models*, Duane

2010 *Due Date*, new father

2011 *Just Go with It*, Ernesto

2011 *Bucky Larson: Born to Be a Star*, Guinness man

2012 *Wanderlust*, Marcy's flunkie

2013 *Hell Baby*, F'resnel

2013 *Afternoon Delight*, Bo

2014 *The Lego Movie*, Foreman Jim (voice)

2014 *Teacher of the Year*, Ronald Douche

2014 *Let's Be Cops*, Pupa
2014 *Horrible Bosses 2*, Mike
2015 *Pitch Perfect 2*, Beca's boss
2015 *Welcome to Happiness*, Proctor
2015 *Tomorrowland*, Hugo
2015 *Vacation*, Jack Peterson
2015 *Hotel Transylvania 2*, Murray (voice)
2015 *Freaks of Nature*, Mr. Keller
2016 *Keanu*, Clarence Goobril/Smoke Dresden
2016 *Don't Think Twice*, Jack
2016 *The Angry Birds Movie*, Judge Peckinpah (voice)
2016 *Storks*, Alpha Wolf (voice)
2016 *Why Him?*, Gustav
2017 *Win It All*, Gene
2017 *The Disaster Artist*, Keegan-Michael Key
2017 *The Star*, Dave (voice)
2018 *Hotel Transylvania 3: Summer Vacation*, Murray (voice)
2018 *The Predator*, Coyle

Producer Credits

2012–2015 *Key & Peele* (TV Series)
2016 *Keanu*

Fact Sheet on Jordan Peele's Work

Comedy Troupes

Two White Guys, comedy duo with Rebecca Drysdale
Boom Chicago

Television Credits

2003–2008 *MADtv*, multiple episodes, multiple characters

2008 *Chocolate News*, multiple episodes, Kelvin Melvin

2009–2010 *SuperNews!*, multiple episodes, voice of various characters

2010–2015 *Childrens Hospital*, multiple episodes, Dr. Brian

2012–2015 *Key & Peele*, multiple episodes, multiple characters

2013 *Workaholics*, "The Worst Generation," Mark

2013 *Comedy Bang! Bang!*, "Andy Samberg Wears a Plaid Shirt & Glasses," Tan Fu

2013 *Axe Cop*, "Super Axe," Super Axe (voice)

2013 *Modern Family*, "A Fair to Remember," Derrick

2013–2014 *Kroll Show*, "Sponsored by Stamps" and "The Greatest Hits of It," multiple characters

2014 *Fargo*, multiple episodes, FBI Agent Budge

2014 *Robot Chicken*, "Victoria's Secret of NIMH" and "Walking Dead Lobster," multiple characters

2014–2016 *Bob's Burgers*, multiple episodes, multiple characters

2015 *Rick and Morty*, "A Rickle in Time," second fourth-dimensional being

2015 *Wet Hot American Summer: First Day of Camp*, multiple episodes, Alan
2015 *SuperMansion*, "A Shop in the Dark," Bugula
2015 *Life in Pieces*, multiple episodes, Chad
2016 *The Muppets*, "Swine Song," Jordan Peele
2016 *American Dad!*, "Criss-Cross Applesauce: The Ballad of Billy Jesusworth," street thug (voice)
2017–2018 *Big Mouth*, multiple episodes, multiple characters

Film Credits

2007 *Twisted Fortune*, G-Money
2010 *Little Fockers*, EMT
2012 *Wanderlust*, Rodney
2016 *Keanu*, Rell Williams/Oil Dresden
2016 *Storks*, Beta Wolf (voice)
2017 *Captain Underpants: The First Epic Movie*, Melvin (voice)

Director Credits

2017 *Get Out*

Producer Credits

2012–2015 *Key & Peele* (TV series)
2016 *Keanu*
2017 *Get Out*
2018 *BlacKkKlansman*
2018 *The Last O.G.* (TV series)

Critical Reviews

Key & Peele

"Creators Keegan-Michael Key and Jordan Peele, both of whom appeared on *MADtv*, are biracial, and they're adept at exploring what it's like to negotiate a world that is perhaps a little more enlightened than it was a decade ago, but still not quite post-racial. The good news is that they're smart about more than just race."—Maureen Ryan, Huffington Post

"Key and Peele's biracialism is central to their comedy, but in a far different way than I'd imagined: it is expansive, not constricting, a Golden Ticket to themes rarely explored on television. Like many of the best, most transgressive comics, they treat human behavior as a form of drag, shape-shifting with aggressive fluidity."—Emily Nussbaum, *New Yorker*

Get Out

The film, which shot to No. 1 at the box office, brazenly inhabits the anxieties that surround miscegenation in our still racially stratified country. The movie's sharp scares, gallows humor, and insidious intelligence are informed by the sensibility, and insistent paranoia, that lurks within the hearts of blacks who must navigate white spaces. The film is a major achievement, a work that deserves, in its own way, to be viewed alongside Barry Jenkins's *Moonlight* as a giant leap forward for the possibilities of black cinema."—Brandon Harris, *New Yorker*

"A jolt-a-minute [horror show] laced with racial tension and stinging satirical wit. How is one movie all that? See *Get Out*, from debuting director Jordan Peele (one half of the comic team of Key and Peele), and get woke. This socially aware scary movie takes you by surprise, setting the scene for a slasher flick that's a ticking timebomb. And then, ka-boom."—Peter Travers, *Rolling Stone*

"In *Get Out*, an exhilaratingly smart and scary freakout about a black man in a white nightmare, the laughs come easily and then go in for the kill."—Manohla Dargis, *New York Times*

"A memorable horror flick if ever there was one, *Get Out* starts with a great title and a promising idea—a black man's fear as he walks at night down a street in an affluent white suburb. Then it delivers on that promise with explosive brilliance. Jordan Peele's debut feature scrupulously honors the genre's conventions. It's creepy, funny and scary—truly scary."—Joe Morgenstern, *Wall Street Journal*

Timeline

1971 Keegan-Michael Key is born in Southfield, Michigan, to a black father and a white mother.

1979 Jordan Peele is born in New York City to a white mother named Lucinda Williams and a black father.

1997 Key joins the Second City Detroit and becomes a part of the main stage cast.

1998 Key marries his first wife, Cynthia Blaise.

2000 Peele lands a spot on the Amsterdam-based improv crew Boom Chicago and drops out of Sarah Lawrence College to pursue comedy.

2001 Key moves to Chicago to work at the e.t.c. Theater at Second City Chicago.

2002 Key and Peele meet while they are both performing at the Comedy Swap event at Second City Chicago.

2003 Peele joins the cast of *MADtv*.

2004 Key joins the cast of *MADtv*.

2006 Key and Peele appear in "Weird Al" Yankovic's "White & Nerdy" music video.

2007 Peele tries out for *Saturday Night Live*.

2008 Peele leaves *MADtv*.

2009 Key leaves *MADtv*.

2012 Key and Peele both appear in the movie *Wanderlust*. They premiere their show *Key & Peele*. They meet President Barack Obama after he requests to meet the comedy duo because he enjoys their comedy.

2013 Peele and comedian Chelsea Peretti start dating.

2014 Key and Peele star in the *Fargo* television series. Key is featured in USA's *Playing House*.

2015 Key performs with Obama at the White House Correspondents' Dinner. The last episode of *Key & Peele* airs. Key files for divorce from Blaise. Peele and Peretti get engaged.

2016 Peele and Peretti get married in Big Sur, California. Key and Peele star in their first leading roles in *Keanu*. Key stars in the indie comedy drama *Don't Think Twice*. *Key & Peele* wins two Emmy Awards.

2017 Key's divorce is finalized. Key gets engaged to Hollywood producer Elisa Pugliese. Peele welcomes his first child, Beaumont Gino Peele, with Peretti. Key appears in the Netflix show *Friends from College*. Key makes his Broadway debut in Steve Martin's *Meteor Shower*. Peele releases his directorial debut *Get Out*.

2018 Key marries Pugliese in New York City. Key stars in the major motion picture *The Predator*. Peele wins the Best Original Screenplay Oscar for *Get Out*. *BlacKkKlansman* is released. *The Last O.G.* airs on TBS.

Glossary

adaptation A movie, television show, play, written work, or other artistic work that is remade with someone else's unique interpretation.

biracial Having parents of different racial groups.

cinematic Having the qualities of a motion picture.

commentary Offering an opinion on a certain subject, typically relating to an event, situation, or piece of artwork.

dark comedy A work that has elements of comedy, tragedy, and, oftentimes, weirdness.

discern To tell two things apart from each other.

flamboyant Acting out in an overly outgoing manner.

gender roles Behaviors, characteristics, and attitudes forced on girls and boys at a young age relating to their sex.

impersonator Someone who imitates other people.

impression An imitation of someone.

improvisation (improv) The study of spontaneous acting and creating scenes, back and forth, with other people.

improviser Someone who performs improv comedy.

improv troupe A group of comedians who perform improv together.

melanin The dark brown or black pigment that can be various shades and is found in people's skin.

minorities People who are part of a group that often experiences disadvantage compared to members of a more dominant social group.

mocking Making fun of something.

monolith Something that is big and made up of a single thing.

nonsensical Describing something so silly it does not even make sense.

parody A humorous imitation of something.

racial equality Giving the same opportunity to people of all races.

racial stereotype Prejudiced beliefs about a particular race of people.

revues Theatrical performances that include short sketches, songs, and dances.

satirical Relating to a form of humor or popular entertainment that draws attention to the flaws and transgressions of culture and politics.

sketch A short, humorous scene or performance; a small part of a comedy show or routine.

sketch comedy The type of comedy that includes short sketches and is often satirical in nature.

stand-up A form of comedy where a comedian makes jokes while speaking in front of an audience.

subdued Lowered in intensity; understated.

white supremacist Someone who believes white people are the superior race.

For More Information

Boom Chicago
Rozengracht 117, 1016 LV
Amsterdam, Netherlands
+31(0)20-217-0400
Website: https://boomchicago.nl
Facebook, Twitter, and Instagram: @BoomChicago
Opened in 1993, this comedy group is based in Amsterdam, The Netherlands, and regularly writes and performs sketch and improv comedy in shows at the Rozentheater. Peele was a part of this company when he first started experimenting with improv comedy.

Just for Laughs Comedy Festival
2101 St. Laurent Boulevard
Montreal, QC H2X 2T5
Canada
(514) 845-3155
Website: https://www.hahaha.com/en
Facebook, Twitter, and Instagram: @justforlaughs
This yearly festival of comedy is held in Montreal, Quebec. Key and Peele have performed at the festival playing their characters of Obama and Luther.

National Comedy Center
203 W. Second Street
Jamestown, NY 14701
(716) 484-2222

Website: http://www.comedycenter.org
Facebook: @nationalcomedycenter
Twitter and Instagram: @NtlComedyCenter
This museum, founded in 2018, is the first in the United States to display the history of American comedy.

Planet Ant Theatre
2357 Caniff Street
Hamtramck, MI 48212
(313) 365-4948
Website: http://www.planetant.com
Facebook, Twitter, and Instagram: @planetantdet
Opened in 1996, this nonprofit artist community was started by Key and his friends. It is now housed in a three-story building containing several different branches, including a record label, a theater company, and a film production company. The theater puts on regular shows, and there are workshops and classes for those interested in learning improv, sketch writing, screenwriting, and acting.

Second City Chicago
1616 N. Wells Street
Chicago, IL 60614
(312) 337-3992
Website: https://www.secondcity.com
Facebook, Twitter, and Instagram: @thesecondcity

Opened in 1959 as the original location of the Second City improv comedy enterprise, this troupe's theater is where Key and Peele first met while performing.

Second City Toronto
51 Mercer Street
Toronto, ON M5V 9G9
Canada
(416) 343-0011
Website: https://www.secondcity.com/toronto
Facebook and Twitter: @SecondCityTO
Instagram: @thesecondcity
Opened in 1972 as part of the Second City improv comedy enterprise, this organization stages comedy shows and offers classes for those interested in learning improv, comedy writing, and stand-up.

For Further Reading

Abdurraqib, Hanif Willis. *They Can't Kill Us Until They Kill Us*. Columbus, OH: Two Dollar Radio, 2017.

Bennett, Sam. *Get It Done: From Procrastination to Creative Genius in 15 Minutes a Day*. Novato, CA: New World Library, 2014.

Brown, Austin Channing. *I'm Still Here: Black Dignity in a World Made for Whiteness*. New York, NY: Convergent Books, 2018.

Curtis, James. *Last Man Standing: Mort Sahl and the Birth of Modern Comedy*. Jackson, MS: University Press of Mississippi, 2017.

Fitzgerald, Kathleen J. *Recognizing Race and Ethnicity: Power, Privilege, and Inequality*. Boulder, CO: Westview, 2017.

Friedman, Budd. *The Improv: An Oral History of the Comedy Club That Revolutionized Stand-Up*. Dallas, TX: BenBella Books, 2018.

Haddish, Tiffany. *The Last Black Unicorn*. New York, NY: Simon & Schuster, 2018.

Hart, Kevin. *I Can't Make this Up: Life Lessons*. New York, NY: 37 Ink, 2017.

Hughley, D. L. *How Not to Get Shot: And Other Advice from White People*. New York, NY: William Morrow Paperbacks, 2018.

Johnson, Mat. *Loving Day*. New York, NY: Spiegel & Grau, 2016.

Libera, Anne. *The Second City Almanac of Improvisation*. Evanston, IL: Northwestern University Press, 2004.

Macks, John. *What Makes America Laugh Before Bed*. New York: NY: Blue Rider Press, 2015.

Noah, Trevor. *Born a Crime: Stories from a South African Childhood*. New York, NY: Spiegel & Grau, 2016.

Oluo, Ijeoma. *So You Want to Talk About Race*. New York, NY: Seal Press, 2018.

Quinn, Colin. *The Coloring Book: A Comedian Solves Race Relations in America*. New York, NY: Grand Central Publishing, 2015.

Rae, Issa. *The Misadventures of Awkward Black Girl*. New York, NY: 37 Ink, Atria, 2016.

Rankine, Claudia. *Citizen: An American Lyric*. London, UK: Penguin Books, 2015.

Robinson, Phoebe. *Everything's Trash, But It's Okay*. New York, NY: Plume, 2018.

Robinson, Phoebe. *You Can't Touch My Hair: And Other Things I Still Have to Explain*. New York, NY: Plume, 2016.

Rogak, Lisa. *Angry Optimist: The Life and Times of Jon Stewart*. New York, NY: Thomas Dunne, 2015.

Rothstein, Richard. *The Color of Law: A Forgotten History of How Our Government Segregated America*. New York, NY: Liveright Publishing Corporation, 2017.

Thomas, Angie. *The Hate U Give*. New York, NY: Balzer + Bray, 2018.

Wasson, Sam. *Improv Nation: How We Made a Great American Art*. New York, NY: Houghton Mifflin Harcourt, 2017.

Yorton, Tom, and Kelly Leonard. *Yes, And: How Improvisation Reverses "No, But" Thinking and Improves Creativity and Collaboration—Lessons from The Second City*. New York, NY: HarperBusiness, 2015.

Zacks, Richard. *Chasing the Last Laugh: Mark Twain's Raucous and Redemptive Round-the-World Comedy Tour*. New York, NY: Doubleday, 2016.

Bibliography

Atencio, Peter, director. *Key & Peele*. "Alien Imposters." Aired September 24, 2014, on Comedy Central.

Atencio, Peter, director. *Key & Peele*. Season 1, episode 1, "Series Premiere," featuring the sketch "Obama's Anger Translator – Meet Luther." Aired January 31, 2012, on Comedy Central.

Atencio, Peter, director. *Key & Peele*. Season 1, episode 8, "Landlord," featuring the sketch "Babysitting Forest Whitaker." Aired March 20, 2012, on Comedy Central.

Atencio, Peter, director. *Key & Peele*. Season 2, episode 6, featuring the sketch "Michael Jackson Halloween." Aired October 31, 2012, on Comedy Central.

Atencio, Peter, director. *Key & Peele*. "The End," featuring the sketch "Negrotown." Aired September 9, 2015, on Comedy Central.

Atencio, Peter, director. Key & *Peele*. "Y'all Ready for This?" Aired July 8, 2015, on Comedy Central.

Bosch, Justin. "President Clinton Answering Jordan Peele's Question." YouTube, uploaded September 16, 2014.

CBS Sunday Morning, featuring Jordan Peele. Aired January 21, 2018, on CBS.

CBS This Morning, featuring Keegan-Michael Key and Jordan Peele. Aired October 10, 2014, on CBS.

Chitwood, Adam. "Jordan Peele's Next Film Is Another Social Thriller for Universal," Collider .com, May 3, 2017. http://collider.com /jordan-peele-next-movie-details.

Cosme, Shante. "Interview: The 'Key & Peele' Guys Talk Shamelessly Playing The Race Card & How Comedy Deflated Egos." Complex.com, February 14, 2012. http://www.complex.com.

C-SPAN. "CLIP: President Obama's Anger Translator (C-SPAN)." YouTube, April 25, 2015.

Daily Show with Trevor Noah, The. "Jordan Peele and Keegan-Michael Key—'Keanu' and Cultural Code-Switching." Aired April 26, 2016, on Comedy Central.

Daily Show with Trevor Noah, The. "Keegan-Michael Key—A Final Address from Obama's Anger Translator: The Daily Show." Aired January 6, 2017, on Comedy Central.

Flickering Myth. "BlacKkKlansman—Jordan Peele Interview." YouTube, August 8, 2018.

Fresh Air. "For Key and Peele, Biracial Roots Bestow Special Comedic 'Power.'" NPR.org, December 31, 2013. https://www.npr.org.

Fresh Air. "'*Get Out*' Sprang From an Effort to Master Fear, Says Director Jordan Peele." NPR.org, March 15, 2017. https://www.npr.org.

GlobalGrindTV. "Key & Peele's Jordan Peele on Season 4, the Chappelle Show & More." YouTube, October 21, 2014.

Goh, Yang-Yi. "Keegan-Michael Key Is Ready to Reintroduce Himself." *The Title*, August 30, 2018. https://thetitlemag.com.

Heisler, Steve. "The Stars of *Key & Peele* Talk About Staying Relevant, and Funny, in Season 2." The A.V. Club, October 30, 2012. http://tv.avclub.com.

Holloway, Daniel. "What's Next for Jordan Peele and His House of Horrors." *Variety*. Retrieved October 19, 2018. https://variety.com.

Howe, Elena. "Seven Directors 'Weaponize Storytelling' to Stand Against Hatred and Violence." *Los Angeles Times*, November 30, 2017. http://www.latimes.com.

Jordan, Julie. "Inside Keegan-Michael Key's Star-Studded Wedding Reception: 'It Was a Magical and Perfect Evening.'" *People*, June 10, 2018. http://people.com.

Koerner, Allyson. "How Did Jordan Peele & Chelsea Peretti Meet? They Can Thank the Internet." Bustle.com, September 17, 2015. http://www.bustle.com/articles/111202-how-did-jordan-peele-chelsea-peretti-meet-they-can-thank-the-internet.

Larry King Now. Season 5, episode 8, "Keegan-Michael Key on 'Key and Peele,' Blackness, and Snoop." First aired August 10, 2016, on Hulu.

Late Night with Seth Meyers. "Jordan Peele's Baby Doesn't Think He's Funny." Aired January 10, 2018, on NBC.

Late Night with Seth Meyers. "Keegan-Michael Key and Jordan Peele's Tips for Telling Them Apart." Aired April 25, 2016, on NBC.

Nodella, Matt, director. *Brooklyn Nine-Nine*, "The Bank Job." Aired May 23, 2017, on Fox.

Peabody Awards. "Key & Peele – 2013 Peabody Award Acceptance Speech." YouTube, published December 8, 2014.

Peele, Jordan, director. *Get Out*. Blumhouse Productions, 2017.

Polowy, Kevin. "How One Fateful Decision Led the Dramatically Trained Keegan-Michael Key on a '19-Year Detour' into Comedy." Yahoo.com, December 22, 2016. http://www.yahoo.com/entertainment/how-one-fateful-decision-lead-the-dramatically-trained-keegan-michael-key-on-a-19-year-detour-into-comedy-223946288.html.

Rahman, Ray. "This Is What Happens When Key & Peele Run a Magazine." *Entertainment Weekly*, September 26, 2014. http://ew.com/article/2014/09/26/this-what-happens-when-key-peele-run-magazine.

Ramos, Dino-Ray. "Jordan Peele Says It Feels Like 'We're in the Sunken Place,' Right Now—PGA Awards." Deadline.com, January 20, 2018. https://deadline.com/2018/01/jordan-peele-get-out-stanley-kramer-award-pga-awards-norman-lear-1202264687.

Reeves, Ronke Idowu. "*Key & Peele*'s Keegan-Michael Key: 'We're Racial Referees of Comedy.'" BET.com, September 30, 2014. https://www.bet.com/news/celebrities/2014/09/30/key-peele-s-keegan-michael-key-were-racial-referees-of-comedy.html.

Richard, Tania. "Keegan-Michael Key from *Key and Peele* Explains How He Embraces the Unexpected." Chicagonow.com, July 30, 2014. http://www.chicagonow.com/writing-my-mind/2014/07/keegan-michael-key-from-key-and-peele-explains-how-he-embraced-the-unexpected-the-most-crucial-ideas-we-have-happen-from-a-moment-of-deep-emotion-and-not-necessarily-a-moment-of-deep-analysis.

Second City, The. "Jordan Peele Talks Great Improv & Meeting 'M@therfu*&er' Keegan-Michael Key." Secondcity.com, February 20, 2018. https://www.secondcity.com/jordan-peele-talks-great-improv-meeting-keegan-michael-key.

Smith, Zadie. "Brother From Another Mother." *New Yorker*, February 23 & March 2, 2015 issue. http://www.newyorker.com/magazine/2015/02/23/brother-another-mother.

Stallworth, Ron. *Black Klansman: A Memoir*. New York, NY: Flatiron Books, 2014.

Tapley, Kristopher. "Playback: Jordan Peele on '*Get Out*' and Art's Role Under a Trump Regime."

Variety, February 23, 2017. https://variety.com/2017/film/in-contention/playback-podcast-jordan-peele-get-out-1201994384.

Team Coco. "Chelsea Peretti & Jordan Peele Eloped with Their Dog to Big Sur – CONAN on TBS." YouTube, published February 6, 2018.

Thorne, Will. "Dave Chappelle: Watching 'Key & Peele' 'Hurt My Feelings.'" Variety.com, March 20, 2017. http://variety.com/2017/tv/news/dave-chappelle-key-and-peele-feud-1202012655.

Vargas-Cooper, Natasha. "Talking *Key and Peele* with Series Director Peter Atencio." Vulture.com, January 31, 2012. http://www.vulture.com/2012/01/talking-key-and-peele-with-series-director-peter-atencio.html.

Walsworth, Jack. "Keegan-Michael Key: Comedy Central Star Fondly Recalls His Days at University." *Varsity News*, December 11, 2013. http://www.thevarsitynews.net/news/view.php/851621/Keegan-Michael-Key-Comedy-Central-star-f.

Wenzel, John. "Keegan-Michael Key Wishes *Key & Peele* Hadn't Predicted 2016's Racial Tension." *Esquire,* August 3, 2016. http://www.esquire.com/entertainment/tv/q-and-a/a47286/keegan-michael-key-interview.

Index

About the Author

Vanessa Oswald is a writer and editor who has written pieces for publications based in New York City and western New York State area, which include *Resource* magazine, *The Public*, *Auxiliary* magazine, and *Niagara Gazette*. In her spare time, she enjoys dancing, traveling, reading, snowboarding, and attending concerts.

Photo Credits

Cover, p. 3 Kathy Hutchins/Shutterstock.com; cover background, interior pages (curtain) Kostsov/Shutterstock.com; p. 7 Kevin Mazur/WireImage/Getty Images; p. 13 © Warner Bros. Television/Courtesy Everett Collection; p. 16 Mark Sullivan/WireImage/Getty Images; p. 18 PictureLux/The Hollywood Archive/Alamy; p. 23 Jeff Kravitz/FilmMagic, Inc/Getty Images; p. 25 © AP Images; p. 30 Tessa Viles/© Warner Bros./Courtesy Everett Collection; p. 32 Axelle/Bauer-Griffin/FilmMagic/Getty Images; p. 36 Maury Phillips/Getty Images; p. 40 Frederick M. Brown/Getty Images; p. 44 Danny Feld/© Comedy Central/Courtesy Everett Collection; p. 46 Noam Galai/FilmMagic/Getty Images; p. 48 Yuri Gripas/AFP/Getty Images; p. 51 Kevin Mazur/VF18/WireImage/Getty Images; pp. 54, 73 Jason LaVeris/FilmMagic/Getty Images; p. 56 Emma McIntyre/Getty Images; p. 58 Imeh Akpanudosen/WireImage/Getty Images; p. 60 FOX Image Collection/Getty Images; p. 65 Gary Miller/Getty Images; p. 67 Michael Loccisano/Getty Images; p. 68 Noam Galai/Getty Images; p. 70 Jean-Baptiste Lacroix/AFP/Getty Images; p. 77 Kevin Mazur/Getty Images; p. 81 KH1/Nicky Nelson/WENN/Newscom.

Design and Layout: Nicole Russo-Duca; Editor: Siyavush Saidian; Photo Researcher: Bruce Donnola